Precious Moments

Memories of my baby's first year

Cheryl Pryor

Arlington & Amelia

ISBN:10-1-886541-24-8
ISBN:13-978-1-886541-24-5

FOR

JENNY, JIM

AND BABY JOSEPH

TABLE OF CONTENTS

About this book

ABOUT THIS BOOK

Congratulations! You just had a baby and you will want to remember every precious moment.

Whether a newborn, a baby who is learning to crawl, taking their first steps, or a curious little thing getting into everything while he/she explores the world we all know mom doesn't have a lot of extra time on her hands that first year of her baby's life, but at the same time will want to record and remember each first momentous occasion and adorable little thing the baby does. Due to mom's lack of time *'Precious Moments'* has been laid out to keep it as simple or as detailed as mom would like.

'Precious Moments' begins with the baby shower, the story of labor and delivery, and continues with bringing the baby home, current events, meeting other family members, and tracking your baby's growth and development are all included.

Record the baby's doctor visits and immunization records, and make notes you may want to discuss with the pediatrician.

'Precious Moments' is laid out with prompts for mom at a glance to be able to put the baby's age and date of when her baby first smiled, first rolled over, first tooth, and took that first momentous step. Each milestone will be recorded from birth to baby's first birthday.

These are precious moments and memories you will want to cherish. Take a moment of your time to record these precious moments for you and your child to look back on one day. *You'll be so glad you did!*

BABY SHOWER

WHO WAS THE HOSTESS OF YOUR BABY SHOWER

_____

WHERE DID THE BABY SHOWER TAKE PLACE

_____

DATE OF BABY SHOWER

_____

GUEST LIST:
NEXT TO EACH GUEST'S NAME MAKE NOTE OF THE
GIFT RECEIVED

_____

_____

_____

_____

2

LABOR & BIRTH

WHAT WAS THE FIRST SIGN THAT YOU WENT INTO LABOR

_____

_____

_____

_____

_____

THAT TIME YOU'VE BEEN WAITING FOR HAS ARRIVED!

THE BABY IS ABOUT TO BE BORN

DESCRIPTION OF LABOR AND EVENTS IN BIRTHING ROOM

_____

_____

_____

_____

_____

_____

_____

_____

WHO WAS PRESENT DURING THE BIRTH

_____

_____

_____

_____

_____

STORY OF MY BABY'S BIRTH

_____

_____

_____

_____

_____

_____

_____

APGAR SCORE

_____

NAME OF HOSPITAL WHERE MY BABY WAS BORN

_____

CITY & STATE WHERE MY BABY WAS BORN

_____

IT'S A

BOY   GIRL

BABY'S NAME

_____

DATE OF BIRTH

_____

TIME OF BIRTH

_____

WEIGHT

_____

LENGTH

_____

PARENT'S NAMES

_____

_____

ANY SIGNIFICANCE TO THE BABY'S NAME

_____

_____

WAS THE BABY NAMED AFTER ANYONE

_____

_____

FROM MOM: WHEN YOU WERE BORN AND I HELD YOU
AND LOOKED INTO YOUR SWEET LITTLE FACE I....

_____

_____

_____

_____

_____

_____

_____

_____

FROM DAD: WHEN I WATCHED YOUR BIRTH AND SAW
YOU TAKE YOUR FIRST BREATH I....

_____

_____

_____

_____

_____

_____

_____

_____

_____

_____

WHO CUT THE BABY'S CORD

_____

_____

DAD'S IMPRESSIONS OF LABOR & DELIVERY

_____

_____

_____

_____

_____

WAS YOUR BABY ADOPTED

_____

IF ADOPTED, AT WHAT AGE DID HE/SHE BECOME A
MEMBER OF YOUR FAMILY

_____

_____

NAME OF BIRTH PARENTS IF YOU KNOW

_____

_____

THROUGH WHAT ATTORNEY OR AGENCY DID THE
ADOPTION TAKE PLACE

_____

_____

DATE OF ADOPTION

_____

CHILD'S AGE AT TIME OF ADOPTION

_____

WAS CHILD NAMED BY HIS BIRTH PARENTS AND IF SO

WHAT DID THEY NAME HIM/HER

_____

ANY INFORMATION YOU HAVE ON THE BIRTH
PARENTS THAT YOUR CHILD WILL ONE DAY WANT TO
KNOW

_____

_____

_____

_____

_____

_____

_____

_____

_____

_____

_____

_____

_____

_____

NOTE TO CHILD FROM ADOPTIVE PARENTS

_____

_____

_____

_____

_____

_____

_____

_____

_____

_____

_____

_____

_____

_____

3

AND BABY MAKES THREE
(OR FOUR, FIVE,....)

WAS YOUR BABY A PREMIE

_____

IF SO, LENGTH OF TIME SPENT IN THE HOSPITAL
AFTER BIRTH

_____

_____

_____

MEDICAL ISSUES DUE TO BEING PREMATURE

_____

_____

_____

_____

_____

_____

WHO DOES THE BABY RESEMBLE

_____

_____

_____

_____

WHAT IN THE WORLD IS GOING ON...

CURRENT EVENTS AT THE TIME OF BABY'S BIRTH

_____

_____

_____

_____

WHO WAS PRESIDENT AT THE TIME OF BABY'S BIRTH

_____

WHAT WERE THE HEADLINES THE DAY THE BABY WAS BORN

_____

_____

_____

_____

PERSONAL THOUGHTS OR COMMENTS FROM MOM OR DAD

_____

_____

_____

_____

_____

_____

_____

_____

_____

_____

_____

4

TAKING OUR BABY HOME

WHAT WAS THE SCARIEST OR MOST INTIMIDATING PART OF CARING FOR THE BABY ONCE YOU BROUGHT HIM/HER HOME FROM THE HOSPITAL

_____

_____

_____

_____

_____

DID YOU HAVE ANY FAMILY OR FRIENDS TO HELP YOU WHEN YOU FIRST CAME HOME

_____

_____

_____

_____

_____

VISITORS: INCLUDE GIFTS, FLOWERS, OR CARDS
RECEIVED

_____

_____

_____

_____

_____

_____

_____

_____

_____

THE BABY'S FIRST ADDRESS (INCLUDE CITY & STATE)

_____

_____

_____

NAMES OF SIBLINGS IN BIRTH ORDER

_____

_____

_____

_____

IF YOUR NEWBORN HAS SIBLINGS WHAT WAS THEIR REACTION TO THE NEW BABY

_____

_____

_____

MESSAGE TO BABY FROM PARENTS

FROM MOM:

_____

_____

_____

_____

_____

_____

_____

_____

_____

FROM DAD:

_____

_____

_____

_____

_____

_____

_____

_____

5

LIFE HAS CERTAINLY CHANGED!

HOW WAS THE BABY'S FIRST NIGHT AT HOME

_____

_____

_____

_____

_____

_____

ANY ISSUES WITH SLEEPING OR FEEDING

_____

_____

_____

_____

IS THE BABY BREAST FED OR BOTTLE FED

_____

FREQUENCY OF FEEDING

_____

_____

DURING THE NIGHT, MY NEWBORN SLEEPS FOR HOW
MANY HOURS AT A STRETCH BETWEEN FEEDINGS

_____

_____

_____

IF YOUR BABY IS A BOY DID YOU HAVE HIM
CIRCUMCISED

_____

_____

_____

WHILE PREGNANT EVERYONE OOH'S AND AAH'S OVER YOUR GROWING BELLY AND ARE FULL OF CONGRATULATIONS, BUT YOU MAY HAVE BEEN UNPREPARED FOR THE SLEEPLESS NIGHTS, FUSSY TIMES, AND OTHER ISSUES THAT MAY COME AS A SURPRISE TO NEW PARENTS. IF YOU HAVE NEVER BEEN AROUND LITTLE ONES YOU MAY HAVE READ SOME OF THIS IN BABY BOOKS BUT STILL FOUND YOURSELVES UNPREPARED FOR GETTING BY ON LITTLE SLEEP AND NOT KNOWING WHY THE BABY IS CRYING. THEN YOU LOOK IN THAT PRECIOUS LITTLE FACE AND ARE FILLED WITH LOVE. A LOVE SO DEEP IT AMAZES YOU.

MOM: I NEVER EXPECTED....

_____

_____

_____

_____

_____

_____

DAD: I NEVER EXPECTED....

_____

_____

_____

_____

_____

_____

VISITORS ONCE YOU ARRIVED HOME

_____

_____

_____

_____

_____

DID YOU HAVE ANY HELPERS THAT HELPED YOU WITH ROCKING THE BABY SO YOU COULD GET SOME MUCH NEEDED SLEEP, HELP WITH HOUSEWORK, RUNNING CHORES, HELP WITH OTHER SIBLINGS, OR BRING ING MEALS

_____

_____

_____

_____

_____

_____

WHAT WERE THE GRANDPARENTS RESPONSE WHEN THEY SAW THE BABY

MATERNAL:

_____

_____

_____

_____

_____

_____

PATERNAL:

_____

_____

_____

_____

_____

_____

WHAT SEEMS TO SOOTHE YOUR BABY WHEN HE/SHE IS FUSSY

_____

_____

6

DOCTOR VISITS

NAME OF PEDIATRICIAN

_____

_____

ADDRESS & CONTACT INFO FOR PEDIATRICIAN

_____

_____

HOW DID YOU CHOOSE YOUR PEDIATRICIAN

_____

_____

FIRST YEAR VISITS TO PEDIATRICIAN

LIST DATE & TIME OF APPOINTMENT FOR EACH VISIT

BIRTH

_____

_____

ONE MONTH

_____

_____

TWO MONTHS

_____

_____

FOUR MONTHS

_____

_____

SIX MONTHS

_____

_____

NINE MONTHS

_____

_____

ONE YEAR

_____

_____

COMMENTS FROM MOM OR DAD:

_____

_____

_____

_____

_____

_____

_____

_____

_____

_____

WEIGHT & GROWTH CHART

BIRTH (WHILE AT THE HOSPITAL)

_____

_____

2 DAYS AFTER GOING HOME YOU MAY HAVE YOUR FIRST PEDIATRICIAN APPOINTMENT

_____

_____

2 WEEKS - ONE MONTH

_____

_____

TWO MONTHS

_____

_____

FOUR MONTHS

_____

_____

SIX MONTHS

_____

_____

NINE MONTHS

_____

_____

ONE YEAR

_____

_____

CONCERNS OR THOUGHTS YOU HAVE ON THE BABY'S WEIGHT OR GROWTH OR COMMENTS THE DOCTOR HAS MADE

_____

_____

_____

_____

_____

_____

_____

VACCINATION RECORDS

LIST DATE RECEIVED & ANY REACTIONS

BIRTH: *HEP B*

_____

_____

ONE – TWO MONTHS: *HEP B*

_____

_____

TWO MONTHS: *DTAP, IPV, HIB, PCV, ROATVIRUS*

_____

_____

FOUR MONTHS: *DTAP, IPV, HIB, PCV, ROTAVIRUS*

_____

_____

SIX MONTHS: *DTAP, HIB, PCV, ROTAVIRUS, INFLUENZA*

_____

SIX MONTHS & UP: *IPV, HEP B*

_____

_____

TWELVE – FIFTEEN MONTHS: *MMR, HIB, HEP B, PCV, HEP A*

_____

_____

BABY'S BLOOD TYPE

_____

_____

MEDICAL HISTORY

MATERNAL SIDE OF THE FAMILY

_____

_____

_____

_____

_____

MEDICAL HISTORY

PATERNAL SIDE OF THE FAMILY

_____

_____

_____

_____

_____

_____

ADDITIONAL COMMENTS:

_____

_____

_____

_____

_____

_____

_____

7

CHOW TIME

YOU MAY FIND IT A GOOD IDEA, AT LEAST INITIALLY WHEN YOU BRING THE BABY HOME, TO KEEP TRACK OF HOW OFTEN YOUR BABY IS NURSING OR BOTTLE FEEDING

THIS DOESN'T HAVE TO BE DONE ON A DAILY BASIS AS MOMS WITH NEWBORNS AND INFANTS HAVE LITTLE ENOUGH TIME AS IT IS.

EVEN IF YOU KEEP TRACK EVERY FEW DAYS FOR AWHILE, OR AS YOU FEEL IS NEEDED, THEN YOU WILL HAVE THIS INFORMATION IF YOUR DOCTOR ASKS AND ALSO TO GIVE YOU AN IDEA IF HE/SHE IS STICKING TO A SCHEDULE.

YOU MAY FIND TO MAKE THINGS EASIER KEEP THIS BOOK NEAR WHERE YOU NURSE THE BABY WITH A CLOCK WITHIN VIEW AND YOU CAN JUST JOT DOWN THE TIME AS YOU ARE NURSING

FEEDING CHART

NEWBORN

_____

_____

_____

_____

_____

_____

_____

_____

_____

_____

_____

_____

_____

TWO WEEKS OF AGE

_____

_____

_____

_____

_____

_____

_____

_____

_____

_____

ONE MONTH

_____

_____

_____

_____

_____

TWO MONTHS

_____

_____

_____

_____

_____

_____

THREE MONTHS

_____

_____

_____

_____

_____

_____

MOTHER'S THOUGHTS, CONCERNS, OR COMMENTS ON THE BABY'S FEEDING

_____

_____

_____

_____

AT WHAT AGE DID THE BABY FIRST EAT SOLIDS

_____

_____

WHAT WAS HIS/HER FIRST SOLID FOOD

_____

_____

WHAT WAS HIS/HER REACTION TO SOLIDS

_____

_____

FAVORITE SOLIDS

_____

_____

AT WHAT AGE DID HE/SHE FIRST DRINK FROM A SIPPY CUP

_____

_____

8

SO I DON'T FORGET, I BETTER WRITE THIS DOWN

WITH LITTLE SLEEP, TRYING TO KEEP UP THE HOUSE, TAKE CARE OF THE BABY AND THE REST OF THE FAMILY, YOU MAY FEEL BRAIN DEAD AT TIMES. IT IS ALWAYS BEST AT THE TIME A QUESTION OR CONCERN OCCURS TO YOU TO WRITE IT DOWN SO YOU DON'T LATER ASK YOURSELF ON THE WAY TO THE DOCTOR'S OFFICE WHAT IT WAS YOU WANTED TO ASK HIM ABOUT. MAKE NOTE OF THE DATE AS YOU WRITE THE QUESTION OR COMMENTS.

QUESTIONS I WANT TO ASK THE DOCTOR

_____

_____

_____

_____

_____

_____

_____

_____

_____

_____

_____

QUESTIONS OR CONCERNS I HAVE ABOUT NURSING I MAY WANT TO TALK TO SOMEONE ABOUT

_____

_____

_____

_____

_____

_____

_____

_____

_____

MY NOTES ON WHEN THE BABY RAN A FEVER, WAS EXTRA FUSSY, OR CONCERNS TO KEEP TRACK OF

_____

_____

_____

_____

_____

_____

_____

_____

_____

_____

RANDOM THOUGHTS & COMMENTS I HAVE

_____

_____

_____

_____

9

RELIGIOUS

WHERE WE ATTEND CHURCH

_____

_____

_____

WHAT DENOMINATION OR FAITH WE BELONG TO, IF
ANY

_____

_____

OUR BABY'S GODPARENTS

_____

_____

WE CHOSE THEM AS GODPARENTS BECAUSE

_____

_____

_____

DATE & PLACE OF BAPTISM

_____

_____

_____

10

KEEPING TRACK OF OUR BABY'S DEVELOPMENT

THE TIME FRAME WILL VARY FROM ONE BABY TO ANOTHER ON THEIR DEVELPMENTAL ACHIEVEMENTS, AND IT CAN CAUSE UNDUE STRESS IF YOU WORRY BECAUSE YOUR BABY'S SIBLING OR YOUR FRIEND'S BABY HAS ALREADY MASTERED AN ACHIEVEMENT THAT YOUR BABY HASN'T. YOUR BABY WILL TOO IN HIS/HER OWN DUE TIME.

RELAX AND ENJOY THIS TIME AND REJOICE WITH EACH NEW EXCITING ACCOMPLISHMENT YOUR BABY ACHIEVES.

LIST AGE AND DATE OF EACH ACCOMPLISHMENT

FOLLOWED MOM & DAD'S MOVEMENTS

_____

_____

LOOKED AT YOUR FACE AS YOU SPOKE TO HIM/HER

_____

_____

LIFTED HEAD FOR A SHORT TIME WHEN PLACED ON HIS/HER STOMACH

_____

_____

MADE A COOING SOUND

_____

_____

SMILES

_____

_____

FIRST NOTICED HIS/HER HANDS

_____

_____

BROUGHT HIS/HER HANDS TOGETHER

_____

_____

HELD ONTO A TOY

_____

_____

HELD HIS/HER HEAD UP ON HIS/HER OWN

_____

_____

LYING ON HIS/HER STOMACH, SUPPORTED THEMSELVES ON THEIR ARMS AND PUSHED THEIR CHEST UP OFF THE GROUND

_____

_____

LAUGHED

_____

_____

FIRST FOUND AND PLAYED WITH HIS FINGERS

_____

_____

FIRST FOUND AND GRABBED HIS TOES

_____

_____

LIFTED HIS HEAD AND TURNED HIS HEAD FROM ONE
SIDE TO THE OTHER

_____

_____

FOLLOWS AN OBJECT WITH HIS EYES

_____

_____

ROLLED OVER:

STOMACH TO BACK

_____

_____

BACK TO STOMACH

_____

_____

TURNED HIS HEAD IN THE DIRECTION OF MOM OR DAD'S VOICE

_____

_____

HOLDS HIS/HER HEAD UPRIGHT ON HIS OWN WHILE BEING HELD

_____

_____

PASSED A TOY FROM ONE HAND TO THE OTHER

_____

_____

PLAYS WITH HIS/HER FINGERS OR TOES

_____

_____

AT WHAT AGE DID HE/SHE TRY TO HELP HOLD THE BOTTLE WHILE BEING FED

_____

_____

FIRST REACHED FOR AND TRIED TO GRAB A TOY

_____

_____

SAT WITH SUPPORT

_____

_____

SOCIAL: FIRST PLAYS PEEK-A-BOO

_____

_____

BEGAN TO SCOOT, CRUISE, OR ATTEMPTED TO CRAWL

_____

_____

MASTERED CRAWLING

_____

FIRST LEARNED TO WAVE BYE-BYE

_____

_____

SAT WITHOUT SUPPORT

_____

_____

FIRST SAT UP ON HIS/HER OWN, FROM LYING ON HIS/HER STOMACH TO A SITTING POSITION

_____

_____

FIRST RESPONDED TO HIS/HER NAME

_____

_____

BEGAN TEETHING

_____

_____

FIRST TOOTH

_____

_____

WAS THE FIRST TOOTH ON THE TOP OR BOTTOM

_____

_____

BEGAN EATING SOLIDS

_____

_____

STANDS HOLDING ONTO FURNITURE

_____

_____

STOOD ON HIS/HER OWN

_____

_____

FIRST BEGIN TAKING STEPS WHILE HOLDING ONTO YOUR HANDS

_____

TAKES HIS/HER FIRST STEPS ON HIS/HER OWN

_____

_____

WALKING ON HIS/HER OWN

_____

_____

FIRST SLEPT THROUGH THE NIGHT

_____

_____

SAID MAMA OR DADA

_____

_____

BEGAN FEEDING HIMSELF/HERSELF FINGER FOODS

_____

_____

POINT AT AN ITEM HE/SHE WANTED

_____

_____

WHEN DID HE/SHE FIRST RAISE HIS/HER ARMS TO BE PICKED UP

_____

_____

FIRST WORD

_____

_____

MOM OR DAD'S COMMENTS ON THESE MILESTONES ACHIEVED

_____

_____

_____

_____

_____

_____

_____

11

LIFE WITH OUR BABY

OTHER THAN A VISIT TO THE PEDIATRICIAN, WHERE
WAS BABY'S FIRST OUTING?

_____

_____

_____

HOW OLD WAS HE/SHE WHEN HE/SHE WENT ON
FIRST OUTING

_____

_____

HOW DID HE/SHE DO

_____

_____

_____

HOW DOES YOUR BABY REACT TO STRANGERS

ONE MONTH: _____

TWO MONTHS: _____

THREE MONTHS: _____

FOUR MONTHS: _____

FIVE MONTHS: _____

SIX MONTHS: _____

SEVEN MONTHS: _____

EIGHT MONTHS: _____

NINE MONTHS: _____

TEN MONTHS: _____

ELEVEN MONTHS: _____

ONE YEAR: _____

WHO WAS THE BABY'S FIRST BABYSITTER

_____

_____

ONCE HE/SHE STARTED EATING SOLIDS, WHAT WERE HIS/HER FAVORITE FOODS

_____

_____

_____

WHAT IS YOUR BABY'S FAVORITE FINGER FOODS

_____

_____

YOUR BABY FINALLY SLEPT THROUGH THE NIGHT AT WHAT AGE

_____

_____

WHAT WAS YOUR BABY'S FAVORITE TOY ONCE HE/SHE WAS MOBILE AND COULD CHOOSE WHAT HE/SHE PLAYED WITH

_____

_____

AT WHAT AGE DID YOUR BABY UNDERSTAND THE WORD 'NO'

_____

_____

HOW DID HE/SHE RESPOND WHEN HE/SHE WAS TOLD 'NO'

_____

_____

IF YOUR BABY WAS BREAST FED, AT WHAT AGE WAS HE/SHE WEANED

_____

_____

AT WHAT AGE WAS THE BABY WHEN YOU WENT ON HIS/HER FIRST VACATION

_____

_____

WOULD YOU DESCRIBE THE TRIP:

A JOY   WE WON'T DO THAT AGAIN FOR AWHILE!

MORE WORK THAN ENJOYMENT   HE/SHE WAS A
                                 GOOD TRAVELER

12

FIRST BIRTHDAY

HOW DID YOU CELEBRATE YOUR BABY'S FIRST
BIRTHDAY

_____

_____

_____

_____

_____

_____

_____

_____

HOW WAS HIS/HER BIRTHDAY CAKE DECORATED

_____

_____

DID YOU HAVE A BIRTHDAY PARTY

_____

_____

IF YOU HAD A PARTY, WHO WERE THE GUESTS

_____

_____

_____

_____

_____

_____

_____

IT'S HARD TO BELIEVE YOUR LITTLE BUNDLE
OF JOY IS A YEAR OLD ALREADY.

THE TIME PASSES SO QUICKLY, BE SURE TO
TREASURE THESE MEMORIES AND PRECIOUS
MOMENTS!

CHILDREN ARE A GIFT OF THE LORD
- PSALM 127:3

www.ingramcontent.com/pod-product-compliance
Lightning Source LLC
Chambersburg PA
CBHW060049050426
42448CB00011B/2358